The factory of consent

Deciphering mass manipulation techniques

Contents

Introduction to Mass Manipulation and Consent

Mass manipulation is a complex concept that involves the use of techniques and strategies to influence the behaviors, opinions, and beliefs of the masses. It is omnipresent in our contemporary society, where governments, companies, and media seek to shape our way of thinking and behaving.

Consent, on the other hand, refers to the approval or acceptance of an idea or proposal. In the context of mass manipulation, consent is often obtained using persuasion and influence techniques to convince people to accept ideas that go against their own interests.

The history of mass manipulation dates back to ancient times, where leaders used speeches and ceremonies to influence crowds. Over time, manipulative techniques have evolved and are now prevalent in mass media, marketing campaigns, political elections, armed conflicts, and social movements.

There are multiple and varied key actors involved in mass manipulation. Governments often use propaganda to influence public opinion and justify their political actions. Companies employ sophisticated marketing campaigns to sell their products. Mass media holds immense power in disseminating information and shaping public opinion.

To better understand mass manipulation, it is essential to

rely on communication and social control theories. Herman and Chomsky's propaganda model, agenda-setting theory, spiral of silence theory, two-step flow theory, and cognitive resonance theory are among the main theories used to decipher the mechanisms of mass manipulation.

Persuasion and influence techniques are also essential in understanding mass manipulation. Cialdini's principles of persuasion, repetition, disinformation, appeals to authority, mere exposure effect, normative and informational influence, storytelling, and framing techniques are strategies commonly used to manipulate the masses.

Cognitive biases also play an important role in mass manipulation. Confirmation bias, group bias, anchoring bias, halo effect, and blind belief are examples of cognitive biases that can be exploited to manipulate opinions.

The psychology of crowds and collective behavior are also key areas in understanding mass manipulation. The theories of Gustave Le Bon and Sigmund Freud, conformity, obedience and deindividuation, group polarization phenomenon, and online disinhibition effect are phenomena that can be used to influence mass behavior.

Mass media is also a key element in mass manipulation. Concentration of media and economic power, fake news and post-truth, diversion and polarization strategies, gatekeeping and framing techniques, and the influence of public relations and lobbying are all strategies used to influence the dissemination of information and public opinions.

With the rise of social media, new forms of mass manipulation have emerged. The effects of echo chambers and filter bubbles, virality and engagement mechanisms, bots and trolls, algorithms and opinion polarization, and micro-targeting and personalized advertisements are examples of techniques used to influence online behaviors and opinions.

Mass manipulation is also a significant issue in politics. Political communication techniques, the use of polls and data to manipulate opinion, image and political discourse management, gerrymandering and voter suppression techniques are strategies used to influence election results and political opinions.

However, it is important to resist mass manipulation and promote critical thinking and civic awareness. Media and information literacy, the importance of diverse sources of information, the development of critical thinking and rational thinking, encouragement of dialogue and constructive debate, and the role of whistleblowers and fact-checking organizations are strategies to combat mass manipulation.

Definition of Mass Manipulation and Consent

Mass manipulation can be seen as a form of large-scale social influence that relies on the use of a set of persuasion techniques and strategies to modify the opinions, attitudes, and behaviors of a large group of people. Techniques of mass manipulation can vary, ranging from repeating key messages to creating an atmosphere of fear or threat, to using public figures to generate support for a cause.

Consent, on the other hand, refers to the conscious and voluntary acceptance or approval of a proposition, request, or action. In the context of mass manipulation, consent can be artificially obtained through various means such as persuasion, social pressure, or manipulation. Persuasion techniques, such as Cialdini's persuasion principles, can be used to change people's opinions or adopt specific behaviors. Social pressure, on the other hand, can be exerted by the group or community to encourage conformity to social norms.

It is important to emphasize that mass manipulation can be used for both positive and negative purposes. Governments can use it to mobilize public opinion in favor of legitimate causes, such as promoting public health. However, mass manipulation can also be used in an abusive manner to deceive people or promote extremist and antidemocratic ideologies.

Media outlets, interest groups, and companies all have key roles to play in mass manipulation. Media outlets, for example, can influence public opinion by selecting and presenting news with particular biases, thereby creating media agendas that define the priorities of public discussions. Interest groups, such as lobbyists, can exert pressure to advance their particular agendas, while companies may use marketing techniques to encourage people to buy their products.

In conclusion, mass manipulation and consent have a long and complex history. Understanding the techniques of mass manipulation is essential for informed citizenship and the protection of individual rights and freedoms.

Objectives and Stakes of Mass Manipulation

Mass manipulation is a practice that aims to influence the perception, beliefs, and behaviors of a large number of people simultaneously. The primary objective of this practice is to elicit tacit or explicit consent from the targeted individuals in order to have them adopt specific attitudes and behaviors. The stakes of mass manipulation are manifold and vary depending on the actors involved in the process.

One of the most important stakes of mass manipulation is the dissemination of false information and conspiracy theories. In the current context of information overload, it is increasingly difficult for individuals to differentiate reliable information from unreliable information. False information can spread quickly and propagate through social networks and traditional media, creating a climate of confusion and mistrust. Conspiracy theories can also be used to sow discord and division within society, by questioning the legitimacy of institutions and governments.

Another significant stake of mass manipulation is the desensitization of individuals to violence and injustice. Images of violence and injustice are often used to influence public opinion and evoke emotional reactions from individuals. However, excessive exposure to such images can lead to progressive desensitization, which can have serious consequences on individuals' perceptions and their ability to respond to injustices.

Mass manipulation can also have significant effects on individuals' mental and emotional well-being. Individuals subjected to mass manipulation may feel betrayed, angry, and frustrated, which can have negative impacts on their mental and emotional health. Individuals may also develop anxiety disorders and post-traumatic stress disorder due to exposure to traumatic events.

Finally, a major stake of mass manipulation is its impact on democracy. When individuals are unable to make informed choices, it can have serious consequences for democratic processes. Elections can be manipulated through techniques such as micro-targeting and disinformation, which can significantly influence electoral outcomes. Therefore, citizens must be able to distinguish reliable information from unreliable information and make informed choices.

In conclusion, mass manipulation is a complex phenomenon with many stakes. It is important to recognize the existence of this practice and be able to identify it in order to protect oneself. Individuals need to be aware of the techniques used for mass manipulation in order to make informed choices and develop critical thinking. It is also important for governments, media, and companies to demonstrate transparency and accountability in their communication with the public.

History of Mass Manipulation and Consent

Mass manipulation and consent have a rich and complex history dating back to antiquity. However, it is with the advent of mass media in the 20th century that mass manipulation has become a major concern for sociologists, psychologists, and citizens.

In the early 20th century, totalitarian regimes used mass manipulation to control populations. The Nazis in Germany and the Communists in the Soviet Union used propaganda, censorship, repression, and terror to maintain power over the masses. They also used Gustave Le Bon's theory on the psychology of crowds to manipulate the masses by creating scapegoats, evoking primal emotions, and cultivating fear.

In Western democracies, governments also used mass manipulation to influence public opinion. During the Cold War, Western governments used propaganda to demonize the Soviet Union and communist countries. Media played a significant role in manipulating public opinion by presenting a stereotyped and simplified view of the enemy. Media also used framing techniques to present events from a particular angle. In the 1950s, sociologist Paul Lazarsfeld developed the two-step flow theory to describe the role of opinion leaders in the spread of messages.

In the 21st century, mass manipulation has become more subtle and sophisticated with the use of new information and communication technologies. Social media has allowed governments, companies, and special interest groups to target specific audiences with personalized messages and targeted advertisements. Social media has also created filter bubbles and echo chambers, where opinions are reinforced by social validation. Bots and trolls are also used to amplify messages and create false debates.

The history of mass manipulation shows that resistance to manipulation is difficult but possible. Social movements, whistleblowers, and fact-checking organizations have played vital roles in exposing mass manipulation. Media and information literacy is also essential in helping citizens develop critical thinking skills and the ability to detect manipulation attempts. Additionally, regulations and laws can be helpful in limiting mass manipulation by governments and companies.

In conclusion, mass manipulation and consent have a complex and varied history. New technologies have created new possibilities for mass manipulation, as well as for resistance to manipulation. Understanding the techniques of mass manipulation is essential for informed citizenship and the protection of individual rights and freedoms.

Role of Key Actors in Mass Manipulation (Governments, Companies, Media)

Mass manipulation is a complex and multifaceted phenomenon that often involves the participation of various key actors, such as governments, companies, and media. Each of these actors uses different means to influence opinions and behaviors of the masses based on their specific interests.

Governments often have political and social objectives that they seek to achieve. To do so, they use various techniques to influence public opinion, such as propaganda, disinformation, censorship, and repression. Governments may also employ more subtle means to manipulate the masses, such as implementing education programs to promote a particular ideology, using fear to induce people to act in a certain way, or disseminating fake news to discredit specific individuals or groups. It is important to note that governments may also use media to propagate specific messages.

Companies, on the other hand, have specific economic interests that they often seek to protect and promote. They can employ different strategies to influence public opinion and consumer behavior, such as advertising, lobbying, online reputation management, event sponsoring, and celebrity endorsements. Companies may also use specific marketing techniques to influence consumer purchasing decisions, such as creating artificial needs, manipulating product perception, and establishing emotional connections with consumers. It is important to note that companies may also use governments to protect their economic interests.

Finally, media outlets also play a significant role in mass manipulation. Media outlets have privileged access to information and can therefore influence opinions and behaviors of the masses by disseminating specific messages. Media outlets can employ various strategies to influence public opinion, such as selecting topics to cover, shaping how they are presented, and controlling the information they contain. Media outlets can also use specific manipulation techniques, such as creating fake news, disseminating disinformation, repetition, emotional manipulation, and polarization. It is important to note that media outlets may also be used by companies to finance their activities.

It is crucial, therefore, for citizens to understand the role of these key actors in mass manipulation and develop critical skills to identify and counter manipulation techniques.

Media and information literacy education, as well as the development of critical thinking and rational thinking, are essential in strengthening citizens' ability to resist mass manipulation. Furthermore, promoting transparency and accountability in institutions and international organizations can help limit abuses of power related to mass manipulation.

In summary, mass manipulation is a phenomenon that concerns everyone and can have serious consequences on society. It is important to become aware of the different manipulation techniques used by key actors in order to avoid falling into the trap of manipulated public opinion.

Theories of Communication and Social Control

In this section, we will explore the main theories of communication and social control. These theories help us understand how media and institutions influence individuals' opinions and behaviors.

Herman and Chomsky's propaganda model is one of the most well-known theories. According to this model, the media is controlled by economic and political elites who use propaganda to maintain their power. The media focuses on topics that support the interests of these elites, while topics that threaten their power are ignored or downplayed.

Another important theory is agenda-setting, which explains how the media influences the importance that people attach to different topics. The media has considerable power in determining the subjects that are discussed in society, by choosing what is covered in newspapers, on television, and on social media.

The theory of the spiral of silence explains how people hesitate to express opinions that are not in line with the majority of society. Individuals are afraid of being rejected or ridiculed, so they often keep their opinions to themselves. This can lead to a false impression of unanimity, where minority opinions are hidden or ignored.

The two-step flow theory describes how opinions and ideas

spread through society. According to this theory, the media first transmit ideas to opinion leaders, who in turn influence the opinions and behaviors of the general population. Opinion leaders can be public figures, experts, friends, or family members.

The theory of cognitive resonance explains how media and institutions can reinforce individuals' beliefs and opinions by providing information that supports these beliefs. For example, if a person believes that immigrants are a danger to society, the media can provide sensational stories that reinforce this belief, leading to polarization in society and distrust towards immigrants.

In summary, these theories help us understand how media and institutions can influence individuals' opinions and behaviors. However, it is important to note that individuals also have the ability to think critically and resist these influences. The next section will explore the techniques of persuasion and influence that are used to manipulate individuals' opinions and behaviors.

Herman and Chomsky's Propaganda Model

Before discussing Herman and Chomsky's propaganda model, it is important to understand what propaganda is. Propaganda can be defined as a set of communication techniques aimed at influencing the opinion and behaviors of a group or society by using biased, often deceptive or fallacious messages to manipulate people's emotions and thoughts.

Herman and Chomsky's propaganda model is a theory developed by Edward Herman and Noam Chomsky in their 1988 book «Manufacturing Consent: The Political Economy of the Mass Media.» This theory argues that the mass media, while presenting themselves as guardians of democracy and freedom of speech, are in reality instruments of mass manipulation, manufacturing consent, and defending the interests of economic and political elites.

Herman and Chomsky's propaganda model is based on five filters that, according to them, allow the media to produce a conformist and homogeneous discourse that reflects the interests and values of economic and political elites:

The ownership filter: Media outlets are often owned by large corporations, oligarchs, or political interests, who have economic and political goals to defend. These owners influence editorial decisions and media guidelines according to their interests.

The advertising filter: The media depends on advertising to survive, and therefore they are likely to please their advertisers by avoiding publishing content that might offend or anger them.

The sources filter: The media tends to favor official sources and experts, who reflect the views of economic and political elites, rather than alternative or dissenting sources.

The flak filter: The media are often subject to pressure and criticism from lobby groups, governmental organizations, or influential individuals seeking to impose their point of view or prevent the dissemination of certain information. This flak can take the form of protest letters, legal action, defamation campaigns, or boycotts.

The ideology filter: The media often reflect the values and beliefs of economic and political elites, who tend to favor neoliberal economic policies, militarism, nationalism, conservatism, or liberalism. The media can also use stereotypes and prejudices to marginalize minority or dissident groups.

Herman and Chomsky's propaganda model shows that mass media plays a key role in mass manipulation by shaping people's perceptions, attitudes, and beliefs on subjects such as politics, the economy, war, the environment, or human rights. The media can thus influence individuals' behavior, political decisions, economic orientations, and consumer choices by exploiting cognitive biases, emotions, and people's aspirations.

To illustrate their propaganda model, Herman and Chomsky analyzed the American media during the Vietnam War, showing how the five filters contributed to supporting the imperialist and militaristic policies of the U.S. government and marginalizing dissenting and pacifist voices. The media presented the war as a struggle against communism and for democracy, avoiding showing the atrocities committed by the U.S. army and demonizing the Vietnamese. The media also favored official sources and pro-war experts, avoiding giving a voice to war opponents. The media was also subjected to pressure and attacks from war supporters, who used flak to discredit critical journalists.

Herman and Chomsky's propaganda model shows that mass manipulation is not the result of a secret plot or an organized conspiracy, but rather the result of a system of social control and consent manufacturing, which involves conscious or unconscious participation of social actors. The propaganda theory invites critical reflection on the role of the media, economic and political elites, and civil society in shaping public opinion and promoting democracy and social justice.

In summary, Herman and Chomsky's propaganda model shows that mass media is not neutral and objective, but is subject to political, economic, and ideological influences that bias their discourse and presentation of reality. This model encourages vigilance and critical thinking about media sources and content, and promotes diversity, transparency, and accountability in the field of communication and information.

Agenda-Setting Theory

Agenda-setting theory is a theory of communication that suggests mass media have the ability to define the public agenda by choosing the current topics to be addressed and giving them particular importance. In other words, the media have the power to determine what the public should pay attention to, which can influence individuals' opinions and attitudes.

This theory was developed in the 1970s by researchers

Maxwell McCombs and Donald Shaw, who studied the media coverage of the 1968 U.S. presidential elections. They found that the topics that received the most attention in the media were also considered the most important by the voters.

Since then, numerous studies have confirmed the importance of agenda-setting in shaping public opinion. For example, research has shown that media coverage of crime can influence the public's perception of safety, even when actual crime rates do not change. Similarly, how the media covers political events can influence the public's opinion on political issues.

It is important to note that agenda-setting is not only about the topics that are covered in the media, but also about how they are presented and the amount of attention given to them. For example, if the media covers a topic in depth and for a long period of time, it can create the impression that it is more important than other topics that are not covered in the same way.

It is also important to note that agenda-setting is not a one-way process in which the media impose their own topics on public opinion. On the contrary, the media are often influenced by the demands and expectations of the public, as well as by the interests of political and economic actors.

Ultimately, agenda-setting theory highlights the importance of the media's role in shaping public opinion. It is important to recognize that editorial choices made by the media have an impact on what people think and the actions they take in response to current events. Citizens should therefore be aware of this influence and use their critical thinking skills to evaluate the information they receive from the media.

Spiral of Silence Theory

The spiral of silence theory is a communication theory that explains how public opinions are formed and developed.
It was formulated by German sociologist Elisabeth Noelle-Neumann in 1974. According to this theory, individuals have a natural tendency to refrain from expressing an opinion if it contradicts the majority opinion in their immediate social environment. This fear of social isolation is called the «spiral of silence.»

The fear of social isolation is a key factor in the spiral of silence theory. Individuals have a natural tendency to conform to the social norms of their environment and to refrain from expressing their opinion if it goes against the majority opinion. This fear of social isolation can be exploited by key actors to influence public opinion and strengthen their power.

Thus, minority opinions tend to be silenced and majority opinions are amplified, reinforcing the perception that the majority is the norm. This can lead to a distortion of social reality and make it difficult to consider different perspectives.

This theory can be applied to mass manipulation because it shows how key actors can use social pressure to strengthen their power and control over public opinions. Governments, businesses, and the media can influence public opinion by creating a social environment that encourages conformity and discourages individuals from speaking up if they have a different opinion.

A recent example of the spiral of silence theory in action is political polarization in the United States. Supporters of the two major parties tend to speak up in public only when surrounded by like-minded people. This reinforces the perception that the two parties represent the only viable options, while alternatives exist.

To counter mass manipulation resulting from the spiral of silence theory, it is important to promote a social environment that encourages freedom of expression and diversity of opinions. Individuals should be encouraged to voice their opinion, even if it goes against the majority. The media should provide objective and balanced information to empower individuals to form their own opinion.

However, it is important to note that the spiral of silence theory is not a universal law, but rather a tendency. Individuals are not equally likely to conform to the social norms of their environment, and social contexts vary based on many factors such as culture, age, and gender.

Finally, the spiral of silence theory can be useful in understanding how public opinions evolve. If a minority opinion becomes popular enough, it can eventually become the new social norm and change behaviors and public policies. This can happen through the emergence of opinion leaders, significant events, or collective awareness.

In conclusion, the spiral of silence theory shows how individuals can be influenced by the social environment in which they operate. Key actors can use this theory to strengthen their power and control over public opinions. It is important to promote a social environment that encourages freedom of expression and diversity of opinions to counter mass manipulation resulting from this theory.

Two-Step Flow Theory

The two-step flow theory, also known as the Two-step Flow, is a communication theory that highlights the importance of interpersonal communication and social influence in shaping opinions and attitudes. According to this theory, media have an indirect influence on the public through opinion leaders.

In the first step of this theory, individuals are exposed to the media. However, the second step is crucial and involves individuals being more influenced by social interactions and conversations with people in their immediate social circle who have a strong influence on them.

Opinion leaders can be individuals with power, authority, or expertise in a particular field, or they can be individuals who have significant social influence, such as celebrities, influencers, or close friends and family members. These opinion leaders can interpret, evaluate, and comment on the information presented by the media, which affects how others perceive that information.

For example, the two-step flow theory can explain why a

television advertisement for a new product may not be as effective as a personal recommendation from a close friend. The advertisement can inform the public about a product, but it is the opinion and recommendation of a friend that can influence a person to purchase it.

Furthermore, the two-step flow theory highlights the importance of understanding the motivations and characteristics of opinion leaders to better understand the influence they have on the public. For example, an opinion leader can be influenced by their own interests and motivations and may also have biases that affect how they interpret the information presented by the media.

Additionally, the two-step flow theory is important in understanding the influence of media in political campaigns. Opinion leaders can play a crucial role in how voters perceive candidates and their political platforms. Politicians may seek to target these opinion leaders to influence voters.

In summary, the two-step flow theory emphasizes the importance of interpersonal communication and social influence in shaping opinions and attitudes. Understanding this theory can help us better understand the influence of media and the formation of opinions and attitudes, as well as how opinion leaders can be used to influence the public. This theory also highlights the importance of understanding the motivations and characteristics of opinion leaders to better understand the influence they have on the public.

Cognitive Resonance Theory

Cognitive resonance theory is an important concept to understand in deciphering the techniques of mass manipulation used in marketing campaigns, media, and political communication. The theory suggests that people are more inclined to accept messages that resonate with their preexisting beliefs and opinions rather than questioning their point of view.

Cognitive resonance occurs when an individual listens to or reads a message and compares it to their own beliefs and opinions. If the message is in harmony with their convictions, they are more likely to accept it without questioning or critically thinking about it. This can explain why some people tend to only listen to and believe sources of information that align with their opinions and dismiss information that contradicts them.

This theory is particularly relevant in the context of media and political campaigns. Journalists and communicators often use framing techniques to present information from an angle that aligns with the opinions and beliefs of their audience. Framing can influence people's perception of a subject by directing their attention to certain aspects and downplaying others. Political campaigns also use this technique to present their candidate in a way that aligns with the opinions of their potential voters.

A concrete example of cognitive resonance theory is seen in political campaigns that use slogans such as «Make America Great Again» or «Yes We Can.» These slogans are often straightforward and direct and are designed to resonate with the beliefs and opinions of the targeted voters. Campaigns that employ this technique aim to reinforce individuals' preexisting beliefs and opinions, rather than trying to convince them to change their minds.

Cognitive resonance can also be used to explain the echo chamber effect on social media. Individuals tend to be attracted to people and groups that share their opinions and beliefs. This tendency can lead to the creation of echo chambers, where individuals only hear opinions that resonate with their own. This polarization can also reinforce individuals' preexisting opinions and beliefs, making them less likely to question their convictions.

However, it is important to note that cognitive resonance is not always a bad thing. Individuals have opinions and beliefs that result from their life experiences and culture, and these opinions should be respected. Cognitive resonance can be used positively to reinforce individuals' positive beliefs and values or to provide them with information that aligns with their interests.

In conclusion, cognitive resonance theory is an important theory to understand how individuals respond to messages that are presented to them. It explains how preexisting beliefs and opinions can influence how individuals perceive the information they receive. Communication techniques, such as framing, are often used to create a message that resonates with the target audience. It is important to understand that cognitive resonance can be used both positively and negatively, and individuals have the right to hold onto their opinions and beliefs.

Persuasion and Influence Techniques

Cialdini's Principles of Persuasion

Cialdini's principles of persuasion are manipulation techniques that aim to influence individuals' behavior. These principles can be used consciously or unconsciously, and their effectiveness is widely recognized in the fields of marketing and advertising.

The Principle of Reciprocity

The first principle is the principle of reciprocity. According to this principle, individuals tend to reciprocate when they receive something. For example, a company may offer a free sample of its product to encourage consumers to purchase the full product. This principle is also used in fundraising campaigns, where organizations provide small gifts to potential donors.

The Principle of Commitment and Consistency

The second principle is the principle of commitment and consistency. This principle states that individuals tend to comply with what they have previously said or done. Once they have made a commitment, they will seek to be consistent with that commitment. Door-to-door campaigns often use this principle by asking individuals to commit to voting for a candidate or making a donation.

The Principle of Social Proof

The third principle is the principle of social proof. Individuals tend to conform to the behaviors of others. This is why companies use testimonials from satisfied customers to encourage consumers to purchase their products. Social media influencers also use this principle by showcasing their popularity and number of followers.

The Principle of Authority

The fourth principle is the principle of authority. Individuals tend to conform to people they perceive as authorities or experts in a certain field. Advertisements often use celebrities or experts to promote products or services.

The Principle of Scarcity

The fifth principle is the principle of scarcity. Individuals tend to value what is rare or difficult to obtain. This is why companies use limited-time promotions or limited editions of their products to encourage consumers to purchase.

The Principle of Likability

Finally, the sixth principle is the principle of likability. Individuals tend to be more influenced by people they like or admire. Advertisements often use charming characters or cute animals to promote products or services.

These six principles are used in many everyday situations, especially in the fields of marketing and advertising. For example, a company may offer a small gift to its customers to activate the principle of reciprocity or use testimonials to activate the principle of social proof.

It is important to note that these persuasion principles are not inherently «bad.» In fact, they can be used ethically and honestly to persuade people to take positive actions. For example, a fundraising campaign for a charitable organization can use the principle of reciprocity to encourage donors to make donations and support a good cause.

However, it is also important to understand that these principles can be used manipulatively. Individuals can be influenced unknowingly using these persuasion techniques. That is why it is important to develop critical thinking skills and be wary of people who seek to influence us at all costs.

Ultimately, the key to resisting manipulation is to remain vigilant and develop critical thinking skills. By understanding Cialdini's persuasion techniques and being aware of their use in everyday life, we can better protect our interests and make more informed decisions. By being skeptical of messages that attempt to manipulate our emotions, we can become more informed consumers and more engaged citizens.

Propaganda and Manipulation Techniques

Propaganda is one of the oldest and most common manipulation techniques used in modern societies to shape public opinion. It is based on the dissemination of biased, often false, messages with the aim of influencing individuals' perceptions and behaviors. Repetition, disinformation, and appeal to authority are some of the most commonly used propaganda techniques.

Repetition is a persuasive technique that involves repeatedly stating a message to keep it anchored in individuals' minds. It is often used in advertising and political campaigns to reinforce people's beliefs and make them believe that the ideas being conveyed are true. However, this technique can also be used abusively to pass lies off as truths.

Disinformation is another manipulation technique that involves spreading false or incomplete information with the aim of deceiving individuals. It is often used to discredit a person or an idea, or to sow confusion and doubt in individuals' minds. Disinformation is frequently used in propaganda campaigns, as well as in the field of online information, where it is often difficult to distinguish reliable information from false information.

Appeal to authority is a persuasive technique that involves referring to a respected person or institution to strengthen an argument. It is often used in advertising campaigns to lend credibility to the products and services being promoted. However, this technique can also be used abusively to promote biased or false ideas by referring to influential figures.

Other manipulation techniques include fear, emotion, lying, flattery, promises, and the use of stereotypes. Fear is a commonly used technique to influence individuals' decisions. Governments and media can use it to encourage specific actions or reactions by appealing to collective fears. Emotion is another technique often used to evoke an emotional response from individuals and motivate them to act in a certain way. Flattery can be used to encourage individuals to conform to certain norms or adopt certain attitudes, while promises can be used to evoke hope and optimism.

To resist these manipulation techniques, it is essential to verify the reliability and source of information, examine the arguments presented with a critical mind, and question the intentions of those presenting these arguments. It is also important to seek diverse sources of information and confront different perspectives to form a fair and balanced understanding.

The Mere Exposure Effect

The mere exposure effect is a persuasive technique that is based on the principle that repeated exposure to a stimulus, such as a word, image, or music, can positively influence individuals' attitudes towards that stimulus. This technique is often used in advertising campaigns and political campaigns to increase familiarity with a product, service, or person.

The mechanism of the mere exposure effect is based on the

theory of fluency, which suggests that the ease of cognitive processing of a stimulus influences our attitude towards it. The easier a stimulus is processed by our brain, the more it is considered pleasant and positive. Thus, if an individual is exposed multiple times to a stimulus, it becomes more familiar and easier to process, which can lead to a more positive attitude towards that stimulus.

Therefore, people develop a preference for something simply because they have been exposed to it multiple times. In other words, the more we are exposed to something, the more likely we are to like it. This effect has been demonstrated in numerous studies, including those that have studied advertising, music, and art.

For example, a study conducted by Zajonc (1968) asked participants to evaluate a series of geometric shapes. Some of the shapes were presented multiple times, while others were presented only once. The results showed that participants preferred the shapes they had seen multiple times, even though they had no real meaning.

However, the mere exposure effect is not infallible. If the stimulus is associated with negative experiences or negative emotions, the effect can be reversed, meaning that the repetition of the stimulus can lead to a more negative attitude towards it. Additionally, the mere exposure effect can be diminished if the individual is aware of the persuasion attempt or if they strongly oppose the object of persuasion.

The mere exposure effect is a powerful persuasive tool, but it must be used properly.

To illustrate the mere exposure effect, let's take the example of an advertising campaign for a new product. If the advertisement is regularly broadcasted on television, radio, and social media, consumers are exposed multiple times to the product. This repetition of exposure can increase familiarity and recognition of the product, which can lead to a more positive attitude towards it. If the product is associated with a positive experience, such as a free tasting or a promotion, the mere exposure effect can be reinforced.

In conclusion, to reiterate one last time, the mere exposure effect is an effective persuasion technique that relies on the repeated exposure of a stimulus to positively influence individuals' attitudes towards it.

Normative and Informational Influence

In mass manipulation, normative and informational influence are common techniques to prompt individuals to adopt specific behavior or accept an idea. Normative influence suggests that individuals are influenced by social norms and seek to conform to them. On the other hand, informational influence refers to how individuals rely on the opinions and information of others to evaluate the relevance of an idea or behavior.

Normative influence is commonly used to influence behavior. For example, when a company or group seeks to encourage participation in an awareness campaign, they may highlight the number of individuals who have already participated, hoping to inspire others to follow suit. Similarly, brands also employ this technique by promoting popular products or presenting them as socially endorsed choices.

Informational influence is used to shape opinions and attitudes by providing information that supports a specific idea. For example, when a company seeks to promote the use of its products, they may provide positive user testimonials or studies demonstrating the benefits of using their products. Media outlets also employ this technique to influence public opinion by presenting biased information that supports their viewpoint.

It is important to note that both types of influence can be used positively or negatively. Normative influence can encourage beneficial society-driven activities, but it can also promote negative behaviors such as drug consumption or extremist activism. Similarly, informational influence can provide valuable and unbiased information, but it can also be used to deceive and manipulate individuals.

Resisting normative and informational influence requires critical thinking and in-depth analysis. Individuals need to learn to evaluate the information they receive and determine if it is reliable and unbiased. They must also be aware of their own norms and opinions and be willing to question them to avoid inappropriate influence.

In summary, normative and informational influence are commonly used mass manipulation techniques to influence behavior and opinions. Individuals need to be aware of these techniques and learn to evaluate the information they receive to avoid inappropriate influence.

Storytelling and Framing Techniques

Storytelling and framing are commonly used persuasion techniques in mass manipulation to influence individuals' attitudes and behaviors.

The storytelling technique (or narrative) is a widely used communication strategy in media, advertising, marketing, politics, and even personal relationships. It involves telling a captivating story that is used to convey a specific message. Stories have emotional power and are often more memorable than raw facts or statistics. Therefore, storytelling can be used to influence individuals' attitudes and behaviors, as well as shape their perception of reality.

Framing is another communication technique that involves presenting information in a particular way, using a specific framework or perspective. The choice of frame can influence how people perceive an event or issue, leading them to focus on certain aspects and ignore others. Frames can be implicit (unspoken) or explicit (clearly expressed). They are often used to provide direction or orientation to thinking and guide individuals in decision-making.

Storytelling and framing techniques are often used together to create a specific image or vision of reality. Stories are used to create an emotional connection with the audience and convey complex messages in a simple and effective way. Frames are used to provide a direction to thinking and influence individuals' perceptions and judgments.

When used maliciously, storytelling and framing can be

employed to manipulate opinions and behaviors. Stories can be used to create an emotional image that has no connection to reality. Frames can be used to conceal certain aspects of an issue or give a false impression of reality. Therefore, storytelling and framing techniques can be used to manipulate individuals' attitudes and behaviors and shape their perception of reality.

Cognitive Biases and Their Role in Mass Manipulation

Confirmation Bias

Confirmation bias is a technique that reinforces an individual's beliefs and opinions by presenting information that supports their preexisting position, while ignoring or downplaying information that contradicts it. This bias is powerful because it taps into the natural tendency of the human mind to seek out and accept information that confirms its beliefs.

Confirmation bias can be utilized in various situations, such as political campaigns, mass media, advertisements, and even everyday conversations. The media can disseminate information that supports a particular political or ideological position, while ignoring information that contradicts it. Advertisers can use testimonials from satisfied customers to convince consumers of the effectiveness of their product, while ignoring negative testimonials.

A common example of confirmation bias is how people can close themselves off to information that contradicts their political views. For example, if someone has a very favorable opinion towards a particular political party, they will be more likely to seek out information that supports this opinion and reject or ignore information that contradicts it.

This can lead to narrow-minded and dogmatic thinking,

where individuals only consider perspectives that reinforce their beliefs, which can result in political polarization and social division. The media can also use confirmation bias by broadcasting information that supports a particular political or ideological position, while ignoring or downplaying information that contradicts it.

Confirmation bias can also manifest itself through social media, where recommendation algorithms can present content that reinforces a user's opinions, while ignoring opposing views. Additionally, people tend to associate with those who share the same opinions, creating «echo chambers» where ideas are reinforced without opposition.

To resist confirmation bias, it is important to expose oneself to a variety of perspectives and different opinions. Actively seeking out information that challenges our beliefs and opinions, and regularly questioning our own viewpoints, can help avoid political polarization and promote mutual understanding between different perspectives and opinions.

Group Biases

Group biases play an essential role in influencing individuals to adopt certain beliefs or behaviors. Social groups such as families, friends, colleagues, and communities have norms, values, and attitudes that are communicated to their members. When an individual joins a group, they are subjected to social pressure to conform to the group's norms, even if it goes against their personal convictions. This pressure can come in various forms, such as persuasion, ridicule, or even the threat of exclusion.

Group biases affect how individuals perceive information and make decisions. Conformity bias is one of the most common biases, where individuals adjust their opinions and behaviors to align with those of their group. This can lead to groupthink, where individuals do not question the group's preconceived ideas and blindly accept collective decisions.

The group illusion bias is another common effect, where group members overestimate the validity and correctness of their collective decisions, even if they are erroneous or unfair. This can lead to complacency or arrogance, where the group does not take into account external opinions or information.

Group polarization bias is also frequent, where the group becomes more extreme in its opinions or behaviors after discussing these subjects with other group members. This can lead to the radicalization of opinions and wider social polarization.

It is important to recognize these group biases to avoid being manipulated by mass influences. Individuals must think autonomously and be able to question the norms and attitudes of their social group. Educators and leaders should not dictate or shape one's way of thinking.

To illustrate this point, let us consider political or social movements that use social media to mobilize masses of people. Group biases can be exploited by using polarization techniques to exacerbate divisions and differences between groups. Individuals may be encouraged to adopt extreme opinions or reject alternative viewpoints. By understanding these biases, individuals who often overlook them might be better equipped to recognize these techniques and make informed choices.

In conclusion, group biases are also a key element in mass manipulation and collective decision-making.

Halo Effect

The halo effect is a cognitive bias that occurs when our overall impression of a person, company, or product influences our evaluation of its specific characteristics. In other words, if we have a positive opinion of a person, we are more likely to attribute positive qualities to that person, even if it is not justified by the facts.

This effect can be used in mass manipulation techniques to influence people's opinions of a person or organization. For example, if a company has a positive image among the public, it can use this image to influence people's opinions of its products, even if those products are not of good quality.

The halo effect can also be used in politics to influence voters' opinions. If a candidate has a positive image among the public, they can use that image to influence voters' opinions of their policies, even if those policies are not in their favor.

To avoid the halo effect, it is important to evaluate

individuals, organizations, and products based on their specific characteristics rather than relying on their overall impression. It is also important to seek out information from different reliable sources to have a more accurate assessment.

Let's take the example of an advertisement for a beauty product. If the advertisement features a celebrity known for their charisma and beauty, the halo effect can make us believe that the product is effective without even looking at the ingredients and specific characteristics of the product. However, by studying the ingredients and independent user reviews, we can have a more accurate opinion of the product.

In summary, the halo effect can be used to subtly influence people's opinions, but it can be avoided by evaluating individuals, organizations, and products based on their specific characteristics and seeking information from different reliable sources.

Anchoring Bias

Anchoring biases are cognitive biases that are often used in mass manipulation because they can have a significant impact on how we perceive and evaluate information. This bias relies on the fact that our brains have a tendency to latch onto the first information presented to us, even if it is not relevant or reliable, and use it as a reference for making subsequent decisions.

A common example of anchoring bias is the use of

strikethrough prices in advertisements, which gives consumers the impression that they are getting a good deal by buying a discounted product. Similarly, political advertisements can use impactful images and slogans at the beginning of a video to anchor an idea or perception in viewers' minds, who will then tend to interpret subsequent information based on that perception.

Anchoring biases are particularly effective when combined with other cognitive biases such as confirmation bias or group biases. For example, if a person is anchored on a false idea, they will be more likely to seek out information that confirms it while ignoring contradictory information.

To resist the influence of anchoring biases, it can be helpful to question whether the first presented information is relevant, reliable, and unbiased before relying on it to make a decision.

In summary, anchoring biases can be a powerful tool in mass manipulation. By being aware of the potential effect of the first presented information, we can better evaluate subsequent information and make more informed decisions.

Blind Belief Bias

Blind belief bias is an important concept in psychology and sociology as it can explain how individuals can easily be manipulated by false or misleading information.

This bias occurs when individuals accept information as

true without seeking to verify or critically evaluate it. In
other words, individuals believe in something without having
sufficient evidence or logical reasons to do so.

Blind belief bias can be exacerbated by several factors, such
as the repetition of information, the perceived credibility
of the information source, and the emotional impact of the
information.

For example, if a person hears a claim repeatedly, they may
end up believing it without questioning its truthfulness.
Similarly, if a person considers a source of information to be
reliable, they may be more inclined to accept the information
it provides without giving it enough scrutiny.

Lastly, information that has a significant emotional impact
can also lead to blind belief bias. People may be more
inclined to believe information that aligns with their
preexisting beliefs or reinforces their viewpoint, even if that
information is not accurate.

It is important to recognize the blind belief bias to avoid being
manipulated by false or misleading information.

In summary, blind belief bias can be compared to a mirage
in the desert. Just as a mirage may appear real but is
actually an illusion, information that is accepted without
sufficient evidence or logical reasons may seem true but is
not necessarily so. By keeping this in mind, individuals can
be more aware of their own tendency to fall into this bias and
take steps to avoid it.»

The Psychology of Crowds and Collective Behavior

The psychology of crowds examines the mental and behavioral processes that occur when a group of people come together. These processes are different from those observed in individuals acting alone, as members of a crowd interact and influence each other, thus creating collective behavior.

Gustave Le Bon was one of the first to study the psychology of crowds and identified several common characteristics, including the loss of individuality and intense emotion. He also suggested that crowds are easily influenced by charismatic leaders and that collective behavior is often irrational.

Sigmund Freud also studied crowds and proposed that crowd members undergo a process of «deindividuation,» meaning they lose their own identity and merge with the group. This deindividuation can lead them to adopt behaviors that they would not have adopted individually.

Modern social psychologists have also studied the psychology of crowds and identified several factors that influence collective behavior. For example, social norms are an important factor that can influence crowd members to adopt behaviors that conform to the group's social norms. The theory of social identification suggests that crowd members may also adopt behaviors that reinforce their group identity.

Conformity is another factor that can influence collective behavior. Crowd members may adopt behaviors that are in line with social norms even if they individually disagree with them. Obedience to authority is also an important factor that can lead crowd members to adopt behaviors dictated by charismatic leaders or authorities.

Collective behavior can also be influenced by external factors such as crowd size, duration of interaction, and degree of anonymity. Larger crowds may be more likely to adopt extreme behaviors or become violent. Crowd members who interact for a longer period may become more cohesive and more inclined to adopt group-conforming behaviors.

Finally, new technologies also have an impact on the psychology of crowds. Social media and online media have created new forms of collective behavior, such as online social movements. These movements can be highly influential and have the potential to lead to significant changes in society.

In conclusion, the psychology of crowds and collective behavior are important areas of study for understanding how groups of people interact and how collective behaviors develop. The psychological and social factors that influence collective behavior are numerous and complex. A thorough understanding of these factors can help prevent negative collective behaviors and promote more positive and constructive behaviors.

Theories of Gustave Le Bon and Sigmund Freud

Gustave Le Bon, a French social psychologist, developed a theory of crowd psychology in his book «The Crowd: A Study of the Popular Mind» in 1895. According to Le Bon, individuals lose their individuality when they are part of a crowd and are thus more easily influenced. Crowds are characterized by collective emotion and a common consciousness that leads them to adopt irrational and impulsive behaviors. Crowds are also characterized by a charismatic leader who is capable of guiding them in a particular direction.

Sigmund Freud, the famous founder of psychoanalysis, also studied mass phenomena. In his book «Group Psychology and the Analysis of the Ego» in 1921, Freud proposed that individuals who are part of a crowd tend to relinquish their individual self in favor of joining a collective self. This loss of individuality allows individuals to free themselves from their inhibitions and behave in an irrational and violent manner. Freud also emphasized the importance of charismatic leaders in the formation of crowds and their ability to manipulate individuals' emotions and desires.

The theories of Gustave Le Bon and Sigmund Freud on crowd psychology have been influential in our understanding of mass manipulation and collective behavior. However, their theories have also been criticized for their oversimplification of human behavior and their lack of consideration for broader social and economic factors that influence individual behavior.

It is important to remember that individuals are not simply

irrational beings who are easily manipulated by charismatic
leaders and collective emotions. Crowd behaviors can
be influenced by factors such as poverty, social injustice,
and political oppression, as well as by actors such as
governments, corporations, and media who seek to serve
their own interests.

Furthermore, Le Bon and Freud's theories were developed
in the early 20th century and were influenced by the socio-
political context of their time. Historical events such as the
two world wars, the rise of fascism and communism, as well
as social movements and technological changes, were not
taken into account in their analyses. Therefore, it is important
to consider historical developments and broader socio-
political contexts when analyzing mass manipulation and
collective behavior.

However, Le Bon and Freud's theories can be useful in
understanding certain crowd and group behaviors, such as
group polarization and deindividuation. For example, social
media can enable the formation of online groups where
individuals share common beliefs and opinions, thereby
reinforcing their polarization. Similarly, online anonymity can
lead to deindividuation and impulsive and irrational behavior.

In conclusion, the theories of Gustave Le Bon and
Sigmund Freud have made important contributions to our
understanding of crowd psychology and collective behavior.
However, they should be considered in their historical and
social context and take into account broader economic
and social factors that influence individual behavior.
These theories can be useful in understanding some

crowd behaviors, but should be used with caution and in combination with other theories and analyses for a more comprehensive understanding of mass manipulation.

Conformity, Obedience, and Deindividuation

Conformity, obedience, and deindividuation are key concepts in mass manipulation. These concepts are important in gaining a better understanding of the formation of collective behaviors.

Conformity can be seen as a natural defense mechanism for individuals who seek to avoid conflict and conform to the majority in order to be socially accepted. This tendency can be amplified by the group effect, which reinforces existing social norms and values. Propagandists can use framing techniques to encourage people to conform to a certain viewpoint by presenting information in a way that makes it more acceptable or desirable.

Obedience can be considered as a consequence of conformity, as individuals tend to obey authorities to avoid sanctions or to conform to social norms. However, obedience can also be reinforced by perceived authority, which refers to the perception that authority has the right to give orders. Manipulators can use persuasion techniques to enhance their perceived authority and encourage people to obey their orders.

Deindividuation is another consequence of conformity, as individuals may lose their personal identity when they are part of a group. This loss of identity can lead to impulsive and irrational behaviors, particularly in crowds. Propagandists can use mass manipulation techniques to deindividuate individuals and encourage them to behave in ways that would be contrary to their values and personality.

To illustrate the impact of conformity, obedience, and deindividuation in mass manipulation, we can look at the example of Nazi propaganda during World War II. Nazi propagandists used framing techniques to encourage Germans to conform to Nazi ideologies by presenting information in a way that made it more acceptable or desirable. The Nazis also reinforced their perceived authority by creating a cult of personality around Adolf Hitler, who was perceived as a charismatic leader capable of leading Germany to greatness.

Group Polarization Phenomenon

Group polarization is a phenomenon that occurs when members of a group become increasingly extreme in their positions and opinions as they discuss with like-minded individuals. This phenomenon can be exacerbated by social media, which allows individuals to easily form groups based on their beliefs and opinions.

Group polarization can be dangerous as it can lead to conflicts and social tensions. For example, a study has shown that online discussion groups on topics such as politics or religion tend to become more polarized over time, which can lead to a breakdown in dialogue and decreased understanding between different groups.

Understanding the mechanisms underlying group polarization is important in order to combat this phenomenon. Communication theories, such as the spiral of silence theory and the agenda-setting theory, can be useful in understanding how media and social networks can influence individuals' opinions and beliefs.

Cognitive biases, such as confirmation bias, can also play a significant role in group polarization. Individuals tend to seek information that confirms their existing beliefs, rather than questioning those beliefs by seeking out contradictory information.

It is important to emphasize that group polarization should not be confused with having strong opinions or defending convictions. It is entirely possible to have firm opinions without being caught up in group polarization.

To counter group polarization, it is important to foster constructive dialogue among different parties, encouraging discussion and mutual understanding.

Media and Information Manipulation

Media Concentration and Economic Power

In our society, the media plays a crucial role in shaping public opinion. However, this function can be compromised when media ownership is concentrated in the hands of a small number of powerful owners who can exert control over the content that is disseminated. Indeed, when the media is controlled by companies that have specific economic, political, or ideological interests, it can lead to a distortion of information and a lack of diversity in viewpoints.

When a small group of media owners controls a large portion of the information disseminated in the media, it can also have a negative impact on competition and media pluralism. Indeed, media owners often have converging economic and political interests, which can influence how they cover events and disseminate information. This can also affect how competing media outlets are treated, leading to a reduction in the diversity of information sources.

Media concentration can also have an impact on the quality of the information that is disseminated. Media owners may be tempted to prioritize topics that attract the most audience or advertising, rather than those that are most relevant or important to society. Furthermore, cost-cutting measures can lead to a decrease in the quality of information, research, and fact-checking.

Lastly, media concentration can also have consequences for press freedom and the independence of journalists. Media owners can exert pressure on journalists to modify or remove articles that could be detrimental to their economic or political interests. This can have a deterrent effect on journalists' ability to investigate sensitive topics or criticize those in power.

To counter media concentration and the resulting economic power, it is essential to support independent journalists and alternative media outlets that tend to be freer and offer more diverse and balanced coverage of events.

Fake News and Post-Truth

Disinformation, «fake news,» and «post-truth» have become common phenomena in our society. People are bombarded with false information and conspiracy theories that have serious consequences on their behavior and decision-making. In this section, we will examine what disinformation is, how it spreads, and the consequences of «post-truth» on society.

Disinformation is defined as the deliberate spread of false information or conspiracy theories with the aim of deceiving people. The authors of disinformation can be governments, companies, political groups, or malicious individuals seeking to promote their own interests. Disinformation is often spread on social media, online forums, and websites, where it can rapidly spread and reach a much larger audience.

False information can have serious consequences on society.

It can affect how people vote, their health and well-being, as well as their behavior in everyday life. For example, disinformation about vaccines has led to an increase in cases of vaccine-preventable diseases, and disinformation about COVID-19 has led to an increase in the number of people refusing to wear masks or get vaccinated.

Post-truth, on the other hand, is defined as the tendency to accept personal opinions and beliefs over objective and verifiable facts. Post-truth can be fueled by disinformation, as people are more inclined to believe what aligns with their preexisting opinions and beliefs. Post-truth can also be encouraged by social media, where algorithms can create «filter bubbles» that reinforce an individual's preexisting opinions.

Diversion and Polarization Strategies

In this section, we will explore the diversion and polarization strategies used in mass manipulation.

The diversion strategy can take various forms. It can involve the spread of false information to divert public attention from an important issue. Media outlets can also focus on a minor issue and create hype around it to attract public attention, while ignoring or downplaying an important issue. Governments can also organize spectacular events or last-minute announcements to divert attention from important topics.

An example of a diversion strategy can be seen in how some

companies avoid being held accountable for their actions
by creating minor scandals to distract the public's attention.
For instance, when a company is accused of questionable
business practices or environmental issues, they may attempt
to divert attention by organizing a spectacular event that
captures media and public attention. This diversion strategy
is used to evade significant accusations and minimize
potential consequences for the company.

Polarization can also be used to divide the population. It can
take the form of artificial opposition, created to divide people
into two opposing camps. For example, a political party may
be demonized by the media, creating polarization between
those who support and those who reject it, without the public
having the means to judge the party's positions.

Social media can also be used to spread polarizing
information and create artificial conflicts between groups.
Media outlets can demonize a political party or candidate,
thus creating polarization between supporters and
opponents. Then, the algorithms of these social media
platforms can amplify these messages and disseminate them
on a large scale, leading to greater polarization and division.

Both techniques can be used together to create distraction
and divide the population, which facilitates manipulation.

Gatekeeping and Framing Techniques

In mass manipulation, gatekeeping and framing techniques play an essential role in creating and disseminating information. Gatekeeping is the process of filtering information by the media and decision-makers, while framing is how information is presented to influence public perception.

Media outlets play an important role in gatekeeping by choosing which stories to cover and deciding how they are presented. This selection can be influenced by factors such as the preferences of media owners, advertiser interests, or relationships with information sources. By controlling the dissemination of information, the media can impact public opinion and the political agenda.

Framing, on the other hand, is a technique used to influence public perception on a subject by using specific language, images, and associations that evoke emotions and reactions. For example, a subject can be presented from a positive or negative angle depending on how it is framed.

Politicians and lobbyists often use framing to shape public opinion on political issues. They may use emotionally charged terms to elicit reactions, such as «illegal immigration» or «tax reform.» These terms frame the issue in a way that makes the public perceive the proposed policies as either positive or negative, depending on how they are presented.

It is important to remember that framing can be used to manipulate opinions, and the media can play a crucial role in disseminating these frames. Therefore, it is essential to remain vigilant and carefully examine information sources and how subjects are presented.

Influence of Public Relations and Lobbying

In our modern world, public relations and lobbying play an increasingly significant role in mass manipulation. Companies, political organizations, and governments use these techniques to influence public opinion in favor of their interests. Public relations are a set of communication techniques aimed at influencing public opinion in favor of a company, product, or organization, while lobbying is a means of exerting pressure on policymakers to adopt policies favorable to a company or organization.

Companies often use public relations to improve their branding and reputation. They hire public relations professionals to create advertising messages, events, and communication campaigns to convince consumers that their products or services are the best on the market. Political organizations also use public relations to persuade voters to support their candidates and policies.

Lobbying is a form of public relations that focuses on advocacy efforts directed at policymakers. Companies and political organizations often hire lobbyists to influence policies and laws that concern them. Lobbyists work closely with policymakers, providing them with information and arguments that persuade them to adopt policies favorable to their clients.

Lobbying can take various forms, including advertising campaigns, political contributions, and public relations efforts. Companies can also organize events and meetings to meet with policymakers and discuss their concerns.

However, lobbying can also have negative consequences for democracy. Lobbyists can pressure policymakers to adopt policies that favor the interests of their clients, rather than the public interest. This can lead to policies that benefit companies and political organizations but harm society as a whole.

To resist mass manipulation through public relations and lobbying, citizens must be aware of their existence and their impact on society. They must be skeptical of advertising messages and political speeches and seek information from independent and credible sources.

Social Media and the Spread of Ideas

Effect of Echo Chambers and Filter Bubbles

Social media has transformed the way we consume and share information. However, this evolution has also created harmful effects, such as echo chambers and filter bubbles. These phenomena can contribute to the polarization of public opinion and the spread of fake news.

Echo chambers occur when individuals surround themselves with people who hold similar opinions to their own. They may be exposed to information that confirms their own beliefs, without being exposed to contradictory opinions. This phenomenon is amplified by the content recommendation algorithms on social media, which suggest posts based on user interests and interactions.

Filter bubbles, on the other hand, result from the use of filters to select content presented to users based on their interests and search history. As a result, users are likely to only see information that confirms their own beliefs, without being exposed to conflicting viewpoints.

These phenomena can have negative effects on society by creating divisions and tensions between different opinions, and reducing the quality of available information. For example, echo chambers can lead to increased polarization of public opinion, as individuals tend to adopt more extreme positions when surrounded by others who share the same opinions.

During the 2011 Egyptian revolution, social media played a significant role but also contributed to the polarization of public opinion. Supporters of Mubarak and opposition supporters formed separate groups on Facebook, each only being exposed to information that confirmed their own beliefs.

Virality and Engagement Mechanisms

Virality and engagement mechanisms are key elements in mass manipulation and the spread of ideas. Virality refers to the rapid and widespread propagation of content on the Internet, typically through social media. Engagement mechanisms, on the other hand, are the ways in which Internet users interact with content, such as liking, sharing, or commenting.

Social media has transformed the way information is shared and consumed. It has allowed people to easily and quickly connect with a large number of others who share the same interests and opinions. However, it has also created environments where ideas are often polarized and divergent views are excluded. Echo chambers and filter bubbles are examples of these environments that can facilitate the spread of fake information and the manipulation of public opinion.

Social media algorithms also play a significant role in mass manipulation. They can encourage polarization by presenting users with content similar to what they have already consumed, further reinforcing their beliefs and opinions. Micro-targeting and personalized advertising are also used to specifically target users based on their interests and online behavior, further enhancing their engagement with specific content.

An example of this is the QAnon movement, a conspiracy theory that emerged on social media in 2017. QAnon supporters believe in a global conspiracy involving political and financial elites seeking to control the world. They actively share content on social media to attract new followers and strengthen their engagement. This conspiracy theory experienced significant growth thanks to the virality and engagement mechanisms of social media.

In response to these issues, organizations such as MediaWise and NewsGuard have been created to promote media literacy and combat online disinformation. MediaWise is a Google initiative that aims to teach young people how to fact-check and detect fake news online. NewsGuard is a fact-checking tool that assesses the reliability of websites based on criteria such as accuracy and transparency.

Bots and Trolls: How They Influence Opinions

Social media has revolutionized the way we communicate and interact with each other. It has also created new opportunities for malicious individuals to manipulate public opinions on a large scale. Bots and trolls are two examples of these malicious practices used to influence opinions on social media.

Bots are automated computer programs that perform repetitive tasks on the Internet, such as replying to tweets or posting messages on discussion forums. Bots can be programmed to spread specific messages, promote ideas or products, and even generate traffic for websites.

Trolls, on the other hand, are individuals who engage in online discussions by posting provocative or offensive messages with the aim of creating confusion or triggering negative reactions. Trolls can also be hired to support a particular cause or individual by spreading false information or amplifying messages.

Bots and trolls are used in a variety of contexts, such as politics, business, social media, information warfare, and propaganda. They can be used to reinforce or denigrate an opinion or person, create echo chambers and filter bubbles, or provoke emotional reactions.

Their effectiveness largely depends on their ability to go unnoticed. Bots are often programmed to act like human users, using generic usernames, random profile pictures, and replicating human language and behavior. Trolls can also conceal their true identity by using pseudonyms and anonymous IP addresses.

An example of the use of bots to influence opinions is the 2016 US presidential election. Investigators discovered that thousands of bots were used to spread fake news on social media in order to promote Donald Trump's candidacy. Bots were also used to amplify negative messages about other candidates, particularly Hillary Clinton.

Another example of the use of bots and trolls is the Syrian conflict. Governments and militant groups have used bots to promote their cause and spread false information. Trolls have also been used to sow confusion and discredit testimonies from conflict victims.

The impact of bots and trolls on public opinions is difficult to measure, but several studies have shown that their influence can be significant. For example, studies have shown that bots can influence search trends on Twitter, and trolls can affect the perception of online comments and decision-making.

It is therefore important to be aware of the presence of these malicious practices and take measures to counteract them. Social media companies and governments can play a significant role by implementing regulations to prevent the abusive use of bots and trolls. Individual users can also contribute by reporting suspicious activities and developing critical thinking skills to detect misleading content and fake profiles.

Algorithm and Opinion Polarization

The use of algorithms to personalize online content has changed the way we access information. Algorithms are computer programs that use user data to recommend content that might interest them. These algorithms can be used to select search results, advertisements, and social media posts. While algorithms can provide a personalized online experience, they can also polarize opinions by filtering the information presented to users.

For example, YouTube's recommendation algorithms have been criticized for leading users to extremist and conspiracy videos due to how the videos are sorted and recommended.

Algorithms use data such as search history, previous clicks, and profile information to recommend relevant content to users. Companies use this data to customize their content and advertisements based on user interests. However, this customization of the online experience can also create filter bubbles, where users are exposed only to information that aligns with their preexisting opinions. This polarization of opinions can lead to a fragmented society, where people are only exposed to similar opinions and not exposed to a diversity of viewpoints.

Another example is conspiracy theories, which are often amplified by social media algorithms. People who believe in conspiracy theories tend to seek out information that confirms their views, which means algorithms may recommend more conspiratorial content, further reinforcing their conviction. This can lead to increased polarization in society and deeper divisions between different communities.

Social media algorithms, such as those used by Facebook and Twitter, also use user data to recommend relevant content. Facebook algorithms are designed to show the most relevant and interesting content to each user. However, this can also create echo chambers, where users are exposed only to opinions similar to their own, as content that does not match their interests does not appear in their newsfeed.

Micro-targeting and Personalized Advertising

Today, companies and organizations can use advanced technologies to micro-target personalized advertisements based on user data collected from social media and the websites they visit. This marketing technique aims to provide more relevant and engaging advertisements to targeted consumers, increasing the chances of them purchasing a product or subscribing to an idea. However, this practice raises ethical concerns regarding the use of user data and how it can affect privacy and freedom of thought.

For example, in 2018, Facebook was accused of allowing political consulting firm Cambridge Analytica to access data from over 50 million Facebook users to target personalized political advertisements during the 2016 US presidential election. Cambridge Analytica allegedly used the data to target voters based on their psychology, political opinions, and interests.

Micro-targeting involves using algorithms to collect and analyze user data in order to deliver personalized advertisements based on their preferences and online behavior. Companies can target consumers based on their age, gender, location, interests, and even past purchasing behavior. Personalized advertisements can be served on social media, websites, mobile apps, and even connected

TVs.

For example, Amazon uses targeting algorithms to recommend products to its customers based on their purchase history, browsing history on the site, searches, and interests.

While this may seem like an effective marketing practice, micro-targeting raises concerns about the impact on user privacy. Companies can collect personal data about users without their explicit consent and use this information for advertising purposes. Additionally, algorithms can profile users and target them with advertisements that can influence their opinions and behavior, without their awareness.

Micro-targeting is also concerning in the context of elections and the manipulation of public opinion. Political campaigns can use this technique to target personalized political advertisements based on users' age, gender, location, and political opinions. These advertisements can be used to spread fake information, personal attacks, or polarize public opinion.

Users can still limit the collection of personal data by adjusting privacy settings on social media and the websites they visit. Companies must also be transparent about how they collect and use user data. For example, in Europe, the General Data Protection Regulation (GDPR) was implemented in May 2018 to protect user privacy and regulate the collection and use of their data.

Political Marketing and Electoral Manipulation

Political Communication Techniques

In the field of political communication, persuasion and influence techniques are often used to manipulate public opinion in favor of a candidate, political party, or ideology. These techniques are designed to target the emotions, fears, and desires of voters in order to persuade them to make a decision in favor of the candidate or party in question. Here are some of the most common techniques used in political communication:

Using surveys and data to manipulate public opinion:

Surveys can be used to influence public opinion in favor of a candidate or political party. Survey results can be manipulated to create the impression that a candidate or political party is more popular than they actually are.

For example, in the 2020 presidential election in Poland, surveys were used to present the candidate from the ruling party, Andrzej Duda, as the favorite, thus influencing public opinion in favor of his political party. This strategy was effective in mobilizing voters and encouraging people to vote for the ruling party.

Managing image and political discourse:

Managing image and political discourse is a communication technique that involves presenting a candidate or political party in a favorable light. Political speeches can be crafted to highlight the strengths and qualities of the candidate or political party, while downplaying weaknesses and flaws.

For example, in the 2008 presidential campaign in the United States, candidate Barack Obama used the slogan «Yes we can» to promote his message of hope and change. This communication campaign was effective in attracting young voters and encouraging them to participate.

Storytelling and framing techniques:

Storytelling and framing techniques are used to present political issues from a certain perspective. Candidates and political parties can use emotionally engaging stories to appeal to voters' emotions, or frame an issue in a way that highlights the advantages of their position.

For example, in the 2017 French presidential elections, candidate Emmanuel Macron used a citizen-centered approach to appeal to voters' emotions and promote his message of change. Macron presented his electoral program as a narrative, using concrete examples to illustrate his points.

Personalized advertising and micro-targeting:

Personalized advertising and micro-targeting techniques allow for targeted advertising based on demographic data, political preferences, and online behavior of voters. These advertisements can be used to influence voters' opinions in favor of a candidate or political party.

For example, in the 2016 presidential election in the United States, Donald Trump's campaign used demographic and online behavior data to target advertisements based on voters' political preferences. This technique was effective in influencing public opinion and encouraging voters to support Trump.

Disinformation campaigns:

Disinformation campaigns are techniques used to spread false information in order to manipulate public opinion. Disinformation campaigns can take the form of fake news, rumors, or conspiracy theories.

Again, in the 2016 presidential election in the United States, disinformation campaigns were used to spread fake news on social media. These campaigns were effective in influencing public opinion and encouraging voters to support one candidate or political party over another.

It is important to note that not all of these political communication techniques are necessarily inherently bad. Candidates and political parties have the right to campaign and promote their ideas. However, it is important for voters to be aware of these techniques and be able to make informed decisions. Voters should be encouraged to seek reliable sources of information and exercise critical thinking before making a political decision.

Image and Political Discourse Management

Image and political discourse management is an essential part of mass manipulation. Politicians and political parties employ sophisticated techniques to shape their image and message in order to gain public support.

Politicians often hire communication consultants to assist them in creating a positive public image. They may use opinion polls to determine what is popular among the public and adjust their image accordingly. Politicians may also focus on issues important to their support base to strengthen their positive image.

In addition to image management, politicians use all the techniques previously mentioned in the book, from the most sophisticated to the simplest, to shape their message and gain public support.

They can use framing techniques to present an issue in a way that influences public opinion. For example, a politician may present a problem as a choice between two opposing options, when in reality, there are multiple possible options.

By framing an issue as a matter of national security, politicians can convince the public to support measures that would otherwise be unpopular. The use of terms like «terrorism» or «illegal immigration» can also influence public opinion in favor of stricter government action.

Furthermore, politicians can use storytelling techniques to tell stories that reinforce their image and message. Stories can be used to present a politician in a positive light, portraying them as a hero who solves society's problems.

Finally, politicians can employ persuasion techniques to convince the public to support their position. They can use principles of persuasion such as reciprocity, authority, commitment, and social proof to influence public opinion. Additionally, they can also use disinformation strategies to deceive the public and gain their support.

Gerrymandering and Voter Suppression Techniques

Electoral manipulation can take many forms, one of the most insidious of which is gerrymandering and voter suppression. Gerrymandering is a technique used to manipulate the boundaries of electoral districts in order to favor one political party over another. This practice can be done blatantly or subtly, but in either case, its goal is to ensure the victory of a political party by manipulating votes.

Let's take a concrete example of gerrymandering in the United States. In 2010, after the midterm elections, Republicans won a large number of seats in state legislatures, giving them a significant advantage in the redrawing of electoral district boundaries. Using demographic and electoral data, they created districts that heavily favored Republicans, isolating Democratic voters in districts with a Democratic majority.

This had the effect of increasing polarization in elections and reducing the representation of ethnic and socioeconomic minorities in state legislatures. It also led to public policies that favored Republican interests at the expense of the interests of the general population.

Voter suppression is another technique of electoral manipulation that aims to prevent certain voters from participating in elections. This technique can be employed in various ways, such as purging voter rolls, imposing strict voting rules, or eliminating polling places in disadvantaged neighborhoods.

Regarding voter suppression, let's take the example of the state of Georgia in the 2018 elections. The then Secretary of State, Brian Kemp, who was also a candidate for governor, implemented a series of measures aimed at discouraging voters from participating in the electoral process. These measures included closing polling places in predominantly Black neighborhoods, requiring photo identification to vote, purging voter rolls, and imposing strict voting rules.

These techniques of electoral manipulation have detrimental consequences on democracy and citizen participation.
They can also reinforce socioeconomic inequalities by marginalizing certain groups in society.

Resistance to Manipulation and Promotion of Critical Thinking

Media and Information Literacy

Media and information literacy is a key element in helping individuals understand and resist mass manipulation. This education should start from a young age and continue throughout life.

An essential approach is to teach individuals how to identify and evaluate sources of information. It is important to understand that not all sources are equal, and that reliable information is essential for forming an informed opinion. Individuals need to learn how to distinguish facts from opinions, reliable sources from dubious or misleading ones, and strong arguments from fallacious ones.

To facilitate this learning, it is possible to use analogies. For example, one can compare information consumption to food consumption: just like with food, it is important to ask where the information comes from, what ingredients it is made of, and whether it is good for our mental health and well-being.

In addition to understanding sources of information, individuals must also learn to recognize techniques of mass manipulation. This includes understanding cognitive biases, persuasion and influence techniques, as well as propaganda and framing strategies.

The development of critical thinking skills is also essential. Individuals must learn how to ask questions, challenge preconceived ideas, evaluate evidence, and be critical thinkers when it comes to the information they receive.

The use of humor and metaphors can be a good method to aid in the development of critical thinking. For example, the analogy of a detective can be used to help individuals understand the importance of asking questions and searching for evidence to reach a solid conclusion.

Finally, it is important to encourage individuals to diversify their sources of information. Individuals must understand that media outlets have biases and interests, and that exposure to a range of perspectives can help understand issues more fully.

In conclusion, media and information literacy is a key element in helping individuals resist mass manipulation. Individuals need to learn how to identify and evaluate sources of information, recognize techniques of manipulation, develop critical thinking skills, and diversify their sources of information. This can be facilitated through the use of analogies and metaphors to aid understanding.

Importance of Diversifying Sources of Information

In our modern world, we are exposed to a large amount of information from various sources. However, not all sources are reliable, and some may even be malicious, with the objective of manipulating and influencing public opinion. Therefore, it is crucial to diversify our sources of information to avoid falling into the trap of mass manipulation.

Indeed, the diversity of sources of information allows for a broader and more nuanced view of events and current topics. By exposing our minds to different perspectives and contradictory viewpoints, we can develop our critical thinking skills and our ability to evaluate information independently. This can help us avoid blindly believing simplistic narratives or false information often spread through the media and social networks.

To diversify our sources of information, it is important to seek out media outlets and news websites with a reputation for objectivity and reliability. It is also helpful to consult international sources to gain a different perspective on events happening in our own country. Lastly, it is important to follow sources that have a different perspective from our own, even if we do not agree with them. This can help us understand the arguments of people with different viewpoints and find points of convergence.

In summary, diversifying sources of information is essential to develop our critical thinking and avoid mass manipulation. By being exposed to different and contradictory perspectives, we can better understand events and current topics and make informed decisions. Therefore, it is important to seek out reliable sources of information and actively and independently stay informed.

Development of Critical Thinking and Rational Thinking

In a world where information is omnipresent and where misinformation can easily be spread, it is crucial to develop our critical thinking and rational thinking to protect ourselves against mass manipulation. The development of critical thinking and rational thinking involves several key steps that can help us better understand and analyze the information presented to us.

The first step is to question our beliefs and assumptions. We must be open to questioning our opinions and positions and be willing to examine the arguments and evidence that support them. We must also be aware of our biases and prejudices and be willing to question them.

The second step is to seek out reliable and credible sources of information. It is important to rely on sources of information that have proven themselves and are known for their reliability and impartiality. We must also be aware of biased sources and propaganda and be willing to critically examine information.

The third step is to evaluate the arguments and evidence presented. We must be willing to examine evidence and evaluate its reliability and relevance. We must also be aware of mass manipulation techniques that can be used to present deceptive or fallacious arguments.

The fourth step is to develop our skills in logical reasoning and problem-solving. We must be willing to critically examine information and evaluate arguments using rigorous methods of logical reasoning. We must also be able to solve problems creatively and propose solutions based on solid evidence and logical arguments.

The fifth step is to communicate our conclusions clearly and concisely. We must be able to effectively communicate our ideas and conclusions using clear and precise language. We must also be willing to listen to the opinions of others and engage in constructive and respectful discussion.

In summary, the development of critical thinking and rational thinking is an ongoing process that involves questioning our beliefs and assumptions, seeking out reliable and credible sources of information, evaluating arguments and evidence presented, developing our skills in logical reasoning and problem-solving, and effectively communicating our conclusions. By developing these skills, we can better protect ourselves against mass manipulation and contribute to a more enlightened and aware world.

Encouraging Dialogue and Constructive Debate

In this section, we will explore the importance of dialogue and constructive debate in the fight against mass manipulation. It is crucial to understand that mass manipulation often works by exploiting people's fears, prejudices, and emotions, and by presenting biased or misleading information to influence their opinion. To counter this, it is crucial to create an environment where people can freely express themselves and exchange views in an open and respectful manner.

Dialogue and constructive debate can play a key role in the fight against mass manipulation by encouraging people to consider different perspectives and critically examine information. Dialogue can help dispel misunderstandings and clarify points of view, while constructive debate can help identify weaknesses in arguments and improve ideas by confronting them with other perspectives.

However, it is important to note that dialogue and constructive debate are effective only if conducted in a respectful and fair manner. This means that all participants must be willing to actively listen to other viewpoints and consider the evidence presented before responding. Furthermore, the debate must be conducted in a spirit of cooperation rather than confrontation, and each participant must be encouraged to express their opinions in a respectful and non-aggressive manner.

It is also important to create a safe and inclusive environment where all participants feel comfortable expressing themselves. This means that participants must respect each other, avoid stigmatizing the opinions of others, and not pressure others to conform to a particular opinion.

Finally, dialogue and constructive debate must be supported by factual and reliable information. Participants must be encouraged to fact-check and consider diverse and credible sources of information before taking a position. In a world where misinformation is pervasive, it is essential to rely on verifiable facts to avoid being deceived.

In conclusion, dialogue and constructive debate can play

a crucial role in the fight against mass manipulation. By encouraging people to consider different perspectives and critically examine information, we can help create an environment where opinions are based on facts rather than manipulated emotions. This requires active engagement from everyone to be willing to actively listen, consider the evidence presented, and express oneself in a respectful and non-aggressive manner.

Case Studies and Historical Examples

Propaganda Campaigns of Totalitarian Regimes (Nazism, Communism)

The propaganda campaigns carried out by totalitarian regimes such as Nazism and Communism have left a lasting mark on history due to their scale and effectiveness. These regimes understood the importance of mass manipulation in controlling public opinion and consolidating their power over the population. Their objective was to create a consensus around their ideology, eliminate all forms of opposition, and make their worldview the only accepted reality.

Totalitarian regimes implemented highly sophisticated propaganda devices, utilizing all available means of communication including the press, radio, cinema, posters, public speeches, and more. They employed proven techniques of manipulation such as repetition, misinformation, appeal to authority, and emotional manipulation. They also relied on powerful symbols and imagery to leave a lasting impression and gain the population's support.

The Nazi regime in Germany used propaganda to spread its antisemitic ideology and justify the persecution of Jews. The Nazi Party implemented a sophisticated propaganda apparatus, employing posters, newspapers, films, and public speeches to demonize Jews and present their extermination as necessary for the survival of the nation. Additionally, the Nazis created caricatures and stereotypes of Jews, blaming them for all the social ills. They also organized demonstrations and boycotts of Jewish businesses to reinforce their antisemitic discourse. One of the most famous campaigns was the «Kristallnacht» in November 1938, in which the Nazis attacked and set fire to Jewish businesses and synagogues throughout Germany.

Similarly, the communist regime in the Soviet Union used propaganda to justify political and economic repression. The Communist Party spread its ideology through posters, films, newspapers, and public speeches, portraying communism as the only possible path to workers' emancipation and the establishment of a just society. However, this propaganda was also used to justify political repression and the elimination of regime opponents. One of the most well-known examples is the Great Purge of 1937-38, during which hundreds of thousands of people suspected of opposing the regime were arrested and executed.

These propaganda campaigns were particularly effective because they were conducted in a context of economic, political, and social crises, which made people vulnerable to deception and in search of stability. Totalitarian regimes exploited the fears and uncertainties of the population to disseminate their message and strengthen their control over society.

However, the propaganda campaigns of totalitarian regimes also revealed their limitations. They eventually generated mistrust and resistance from certain groups within the population, particularly intellectuals and artists, who openly criticized the regime. Resistance movements also played a vital role in delegitimizing propaganda and mobilizing public opinion against the regime.

In conclusion, the propaganda campaigns conducted by totalitarian regimes illustrate striking examples of mass manipulation. They used sophisticated techniques to control public opinion and impose their ideology. Nonetheless, these campaigns also exposed their limits, particularly due to resistance from certain segments of the population. It is essential to understand these mechanisms in order to avoid falling into the same traps in the future.

The Influence of Media in Wars and Conflicts (Vietnam War, Iraq War)

War is often used as a means of mass manipulation to justify actions and rally public support. The media plays a crucial role in shaping the public's perception and understanding of conflicts, as well as in how governments can justify their intervention in armed conflicts.

Let us take the example of the Vietnam War. The media played a significant role in shaping public opinion and opposition to the war. Images of American soldiers killed or wounded, as well as innocent Vietnamese civilians, shocked public opinion and contributed to the rise of anti-war sentiment in the United States. Journalists such as Walter Cronkite provided reports that helped people understand the human costs of war and fueled the protest movement.

However, the impact of the media on war does not end there. Media also play a crucial role in how governments justify their intervention in armed conflicts. For example, during the Iraq War, the media extensively disseminated allegations, later proven false, that Saddam Hussein's Iraqi regime possessed weapons of mass destruction, which served as justification for the United States' invasion of Iraq. Many critics accused the media of being manipulated by the US government to support the war.

It is essential to emphasize that governments can manipulate the information disseminated by the media to evoke emotional reactions and justify controversial military actions. Therefore, it is important for citizens to remain vigilant and critical regarding the information they receive, exercising discernment and thoroughly examining the sources of information.

Journalists, in turn, play an important role in preventing the manipulation of information during armed conflicts. They must strive to provide accurate and balanced information about ongoing events, verifying them through multiple reliable sources. Additionally, they must be conscious of their responsibility to the public and make every effort to maintain impartiality and objectivity.

Finally, it is important to note that the media can also play a positive role in resolving armed conflicts. By objectively covering events and encouraging dialogue between conflicting parties, the media can contribute to reducing tensions and promoting peace.

Successful Political Marketing Campaigns (Barack Obama, Brexit, Donald Trump)

Mass manipulation is a common practice in the world of politics, where political marketing campaigns are used to influence public opinion and win elections. Successful political marketing campaigns, such as those conducted by Barack Obama, Brexit, and Donald Trump, have been studied to understand the techniques of persuasion and influence employed to achieve results.

Barack Obama's 2008 campaign is considered one of the most successful political marketing campaigns of all time. The slogan «Yes We Can» was widely used to mobilize voters, especially the youth and minorities, and the message of hope and change was consistently repeated throughout the campaign. The campaign also effectively utilized social media platforms, using them to mobilize voters, disseminate key messages, and collect funds.

Brexit, the campaign that led to the United Kingdom's departure from the European Union in 2016, is an example of a successful political marketing campaign that employed techniques of emotional manipulation to influence voters. The campaign focused on the fear of immigration, utilizing slogans such as «Take back control» to promote national sovereignty and independence. Supporters of the campaign also used social media to spread misleading information and fake news, further polarizing and spreading misinformation.

Donald Trump's 2016 campaign is also an example of a successful political marketing campaign that used persuasion and influence techniques to mobilize voters. The campaign emphasized the message «Make America Great Again,» which was consistently repeated throughout the campaign. It also effectively utilized social media, employing tactics such as micro-targeting and personalized ads to reach specific groups of voters.

These successful political marketing campaigns all employed techniques of persuasion and influence to mobilize voters and win votes. These techniques included the repetition of key messages, the use of simple and memorable slogans, the utilization of social media to engage voters, and the creation of polarization to strengthen opinions.

The Impact of Social Media on Revolutions and Social Movements (Arab Spring, Occupy Movement, Yellow Vests)

Social media has had a significant impact on social movements and revolutions worldwide. Its ability to facilitate the rapid diffusion of information and mobilize large numbers of people has created new opportunities for protest movements. However, its role in these movements has also raised questions about how it can be used to influence and manipulate public opinion.

The Arab Spring was one of the earliest examples of social media's capacity to rapidly mobilize the masses. In Tunisia, political activist Mohamed Bouazizi set himself on fire in protest against police harassment. Photos of his burning body were shared on Facebook and Twitter, triggering a wave of protests that eventually led to the downfall of President Zine El Abidine Ben Ali. Social media also played a crucial role in the protests in Egypt, Libya, and Syria.

The Occupy Movement also utilized social media to mobilize and organize protests. The demonstrations began at New York's Zuccotti Park in September 2011 but quickly spread to other American cities and around the world. The hashtag #OccupyWallStreet gained momentum on Twitter, allowing protesters to share real-time information and photos.

The Yellow Vests movement in France was also extensively mobilized through social media. The movement started in November 2018 in response to an increase in fuel taxes but quickly transformed into a broader protest against the government's economic policies. The Yellow Vests used social media to organize demonstrations, share videos of police violence, and mobilize public opinion.

However, social media has also been used to manipulate public opinion and influence election outcomes. In 2016, Russian trolls used social media to influence the US presidential election in favor of Donald Trump. They created fake accounts to spread misleading information, sow discord, and encourage political polarization.

It is important to note that the impact of social media on social movements is not always positive. While social media can amplify the voices of the underrepresented and marginalized, it can also be used to spread false information and manipulate public opinion. Therefore, it is essential to understand how social media is used in social movements and promote responsible and ethical use of these tools.